101
Helpful Illusions

First published by O Books, 2009
O Books is an imprint of John Hunt Publishing Ltd., The Bothy, Deershot Lodge, Park Lane, Ropley,
Hants, SO24 0BE, UK
office1@o-books.net
www.o-books.net

Distribution in:

UK and Europe
Orca Book Services
orders@orcabookservices.co.uk
Tel: 01202 665432 Fax: 01202 666219
Int. code (44)

USA and Canada
NBN
custserv@nbnbooks.com
Tel: 1 800 462 6420 Fax: 1 800 338 4550

Australia and New Zealand
Brumby Books
sales@brumbybooks.com.au
Tel: 61 3 9761 5535 Fax: 61 3 9761 7095

Far East (offices in Singapore, Thailand,
Hong Kong, Taiwan)
Pansing Distribution Pte Ltd
kemal@pansing.com
Tel: 65 6319 9939 Fax: 65 6462 5761

South Africa
Alternative Books
altbook@peterhyde.co.za
Tel: 021 555 4027 Fax: 021 447 1430

Text copyright Shaykh Fadhlalla Haeri 2008

Design: Stuart Davies

ISBN: 978 1 84694 278 5

A CIP catalogue record for this book is available
from the British Library.

Printed by Digital Book Print

O Books operates a distinctive and ethical publishing philosophy in
all areas of its business, from its global network of authors to
production and worldwide distribution.

101
Helpful Illusions

Shaykh Fadhlalla Haeri

BOOKS

Winchester, UK
Washington, USA

CONTENTS

Foreword

The greatest adventure a human being can undertake is the journey from the ego, the "I," to the Self, the divine consciousness that exists within each of us. This most demanding and fulfilling journey takes us from a world of separation, governed by the ego's fears, anxieties and desires, into the experience of divine unity, the oneness, peace and harmony that belong to the core of our being. It is a radical shift in consciousness that unfolds gradually within the traveler, helped by spiritual teachings, practices, and above all the grace that is given. Traditionally it is described as a turning away from the illusions of the outer world of the senses, to discover the deeper truth that is within us. In the Sufi tradition it is a "turning of the heart" that reveals the truth of divine love that is veiled by the illusions of the ego and our lower nature. Traveling the path these veils are gradually lifted, and we awake in the sunshine of the Self, in the wholeness of our divine consciousness.

The outer world is initially seen as a place of illusion that distracts us from this quest. And the spiritual seeker often has to make an intense effort to become free of these illusions, free of the grip of the ego and the desires of our lower nature. We work hard to free our self from the many attachments, the conscious and unconscious patterns that imprison us. But Sufism has revealed a deeper truth that the illusions of the outer world can also be read as signposts on the journey Home. God, the Beloved, is hidden in the depths of our heart, and for the mystic is an unknowable Essence. But in the outer world He manifests Himself in all the multiplicity of existence. The outer world is a reflection or manifestation of divine Truth. To quote the great Sufi, Ibn 'Arabi:

How can I know You when You are the Inwardly Hidden who is not known?

How can I not know You when You are the Outwardly manifest, making Yourself known to me in everything?[1]

The challenge presented by *101 Helpful Illusions* is how to use the illusions of the outer world as guidance along the path without being trapped in its distortions and distractions. How can the multiplicity of creation lead us back to the unity of the Self, the truth of our divine nature?

For the spiritual traveler, one of the most important qualities to learn is spiritual discrimination: how to differentiate what belongs to the ego and what belongs to the Self. The Self is waiting and wanting to help us on this journey of liberation, but we have to learn how to listen to its voice, how to know when it is guiding us rather than the deceptive voices of the ego and the mind. If we can read this book with real receptivity, we will find the wisdom of one who has already made this journey and can help the traveler. Shakyh Fadhlalla Haeri speaks with the wisdom and understanding of one who has seen through the world's illusions, but rather than just dismiss them as obstacles, guides us into a deeper understanding of how they can help us. This is the real value of this book.

Today we live in a civilization where it is not easy to turn away from the world. On every side we are bombarded by a thousand images designed to distract us. The work of the traveler is not to find a place of isolation, to separate himself from the world, but to continue the journey amidst all of these distractions. It is so easy to get lost in the maze of life's illusions. It is the art of a master to be able to use these illusions as signposts on the journey, as a way to develop, or reconnect with the pure consciousness of the Self. Life has real lessons to teach us, from the patterns and flow imaged in nature, to recognizing and

---

[1] Trans. Pablo Beneito and Stephen Hirtensein, *Seven Days of the Heart*, pp. 43-44

differentiating between the needs of the ego and the needs of the soul. But without understanding life's signs, we pass by, blinded by our own limitations and conditioning.

Shakyh Fadhlalla Haeri explores the illusions of the natural world, and the human illusions that we find in relationships with its many projections, also the addictions and collective patterns that determine our values and ways of behaving. And always we are shown how real understanding can free us from their grip and help us to realize the unity of a deeper consciousness. Through these apparent paradoxes we can grow towards this light that is within us, begin to claim what is real. We are even made aware of the higher illusions of spiritual life, which so easily waylay the traveler. Rather than projecting our wisdom and spiritual qualities on others, we are reminded of the sacred treasure within our own heart. The Sufi says that the outer teacher always points to the inner teacher, and that the greatest teacher is life itself. Like a Zen koan, these simple sayings affirm the true teaching that life has to offer; that life itself is a real gateway to God.

Of course it is easy to read such a book and feel its wisdom and guidance. The real work is always to practice such precepts, to take the teachings that are offered and live them in our daily life. My own teacher said that mysticism is to "bear the heat and burden of the day." In the midst of life's clamor there is a deeper secret waiting to be uncovered, to be claimed, to be lived. The test is to dare to encounter life's many illusions with the strength and commitment of one who wants to make this journey for the sake of what is real, for the sake of Truth. Then, and only then, will life and the Beloved come to meet us, and, taking us by the hand, guide us from the limited consciousness of the ego to the vaster dimension of our true Self. This is what is being offered: how to recognize and return to the oneness that is all around us.

Llewellyn Vaughan-Lee Ph.D., February 2009

Preface

The essence of a human being is glorious, but like the kernel of a nut it needs to be prised out of its shell, the self-ego. This process is the awakening to the eternal and boundless soul within the inner heart. In the appropriate season of maturity the self needs to transcend. The seeds of plants perform that process naturally whereas the human has an apparent choice and needs to apply conscious effort to purify the heart and be illumined by the soul. A child needs to develop its ego and personality but the mature person will reflect upon the higher self until the realisation of the perfect soul within supersedes all other considerations. The wise realise that the self ego was only there like a shell to protect the inner heart and soul until the appropriate time of transformation and spiritual awakening.

All Illusions and paradoxes of human experience are part of the shell. Once they dissolve then everything becomes beautifully clear and non-worldly – beyond mental limitations and normal causalities.

This book shares with the reader that whatever we consider confusing illusions or paradoxes are actually conducive to and helpful along the path of awakening and soul discovery. When consciousness transcends duality and recognises all-encompassing unity then all of these paradoxes and illusions are tolerated, for like the shell their purpose becomes clear. We move from outer uncertainty to inner clarity and therefore all outer dualities and agitations become insignificant.

Introduction

We all love to discover rare gems or treasures in life. The human soul (or spirit) is the supreme treasure, hidden and veiled by the ego – the self.

The essence of human nature is an eternal light within the inner heart - a super consciousness called spirit, or soul. This soul is like a sacred hologram that bears desirable attributes and qualities considered universally virtuous and which give rise to human morality. But this intangible soul also gives rise to its shadow companion, the individual self or ego, which grows and evolves towards the recognition and knowledge of the soul and eventually to union with it. Personal individual consciousness is conditioned and is derived from the soul's consciousness which replicates pure or supreme consciousness. Thus it can be said that every soul is a flash of the cosmic soul or God and overflows with attributes of the sacred essence.

The duality of self and soul within the human being echoes all existential pluralities and complementary opposites: the outer and inner, form and meaning, earth and heavens, seen and unseen, good and bad, birth and death, easy and difficult and numerous other states within our inner make up. All of these opposites and dualities are experienced by us and are mirrored in the outer world. Thus the human being is a microcosm resonating with the macrocosm, and reflects the unifying field and one reality or truth that holds the universal realities.

Consciousness has numerous levels and spheres. Lower consciousness is basic and life giving. This gives rise to a local, conditioned and personal awareness to animated creatures. Higher consciousness, however, is exclusive to human beings. This is often called pure, divine, supreme or God-consciousness. Lower consciousness is an aspect of higher consciousness and is dependent upon it.

3

Conditioned human consciousness evolves with age and wisdom, towards higher levels until there is unison between the self (ego) and soul, through the inner heart. This unified consciousness is sometimes called enlightenment or spiritual awakening. The human soul is like a sacred spark representing the cosmic soul or God within the human kingdom of body, mind and intellect.

The human journey and growth is both physical as well as spiritual. The physical or biological part is governed to a great extent by genes, as well as the environment. Spiritual growth follows alongside physiological and psychological maturity. Self-realisation or enlightenment brings about personal contentment, peace and joy without negating the ever-changing outer realities.

Life's journey is an adventure to discover inner and outer perfection and then to discern true goodness in every situation. The purpose of all worldly challenges is to discover the ever-present sacred essence that permeates the universe through knowledge of the soul within our heart. Terms like 'humanity', 'unity' and even mundane 'relationships' reflect different levels of the unique Oneness of the cosmic essence, which manifests and appears as diverse dualities and pluralities, gross and subtle.

Space–time is the nursery wherein all possible creations occur and manifest as interaction between energy and matter in a natural cyclical fashion, with births and deaths signifying beginnings and ends of particular events. This nursery provides local and broader boundaries so that entities experience individuality due to conditioned consciousness relating to survival, growth and ongoingness. This is the cause of egotistic conduct for survival and growth.

This basic level of consciousness appears as separate from higher consciousness due to the self delusion of its independence and willfulness. However, human beings have the potential to transcend to a higher soul consciousness where self and soul are in unison and end the illusion of separation and confinement of space to time. This breakthrough leads to the realisation of cosmic unity and eternal oneness in essence, which permeates the universe.

There are two levels of human evolution and growth. One involves physical and mental maturity with the development of certain uniqueness about each individual. The second level is spiritual evolvement and the realisation of higher consciousness, and the falsehood of all earthly events and experiences which are initially helpful for survival, but become barriers to soul consciousness and thereby lasting relief and contentment.

The human drive for wellbeing, harmony and happiness and avoidance of sickness, discord and misery can be a great force to realise the source and essence of life – the free and joyful soul within. The human soul is ever-free, content and stable, and is not subject to the changing world of duality, insecurity and uncertainty experienced by the ego-self.

What starts as a selfish, egocentric and conditioned but evolving personality is in fact necessary for our early development but becomes an obstacle and handicap with regard to higher consciousness and liberation from all worldly mental boundaries. We spend the first half of our life learning skills to act, gather and achieve outer objectives. This process is a prelude to the wisdom that success and failure are never separate and that pleasure and pain are twin companions, appearing as opposites. Mind and intellect become sharp and focused but the 'soul-mate vacancy' may persist. Through spiritual wisdom the self will eventually learn to submit to the soul and thereby rest in perfect unison and contentment. This state represents the final purpose of human life.

In truth, the self and soul are never separate except that the ego is acting as the shadow companion of the soul, desiring all the soul's qualities and blissful state, but is distracted by the illusion of its independence as a separate and worthy entity.

Self delusions are the result of the illusion that the self is real on its own and is free of the soul. Until the self discovers its own resident master within the heart it remains restless and hapless – moving from one delusion to another. Anger, disappointment, denial and other so-called 'negative' emotions are due to the self being distracted from yielding to soul attraction and the original primal addiction to it. The soul is broadcasting its unconditional love to the self, which avoids acknowledgement of its dependence upon the soul. Self importance, distractions and the ever-changing roles and identities continue until at last, through shocks and divine grace, it may surrender and awaken to this sacred call and embrace. This is the union worth celebrating on earth whose decree was written in heaven.

A spiritually insightful person will discover that all so-called faults, vices or negative traits belong to the ego-self while all perfection and virtues are attributes of the soul; and it is these higher qualities and ideals that have been beckoning us all along. Guilt and neglect arise due to the discrepancy between what a person *could* have done and what was *actually* done. Mistakes occur due to the lack of self awareness or presence of mind and heart at the time of action. This is why an apologetic person may say 'I was beside myself', or 'it wasn't really me who did that' or 'I don't know what came over me'. So who is the real 'me'? A better version than the usual! A self that refers to the soul?!

The restless self may fall through to greater distraction, confusion and self-delusion or surrender to a more harmonious and wholesome state by sensitive understanding of the signs of the soul. This state of heartful awareness of the 'higher self', or consciousness, is a natural state as the soul is the essence of life.

If illusions cause the seeker of truth to suffer then it is a healthy warning to retract from inappropriateness and to re-focus and follow the illumined map leading to inner liberty and harmony. Vices can be keys to virtues and illusions can lead towards illumined conclusions.

To recognise personal illusions, traps and biases and to go

beyond them is the necessary step towards awakening to the ever-present truth and bliss. This outcome is what we describe as a fulfilled life. What was early on a selfish act justified as intelligent self-interest is now replaced with 'soul' interest - far more durable and reliable. Enlightenment is the outcome of an evolution from basic personal need for survival and growth to pure consciousness. It is a metamorphosis from the dark cocoon of delusion to the ever-present garden of light and delight.

This book highlights natural veils waiting to be transcended by disciplined courage, wisdom and insight. Everything in creation has a purpose relevant to specific situation that could lead the seeker of higher knowledge towards the ultimate spiritual truth of oneness. Thus our egotistic vices can indeed be stepping stones towards acting selflessly, spontaneously, and cheerfully with heightened awareness and good expectations in all situations. Indeed, all our mistakes can lead us towards the desired spiritual awakening – the ultimate purpose in life: experiencing and knowing the universal oneness.

Chapter 1

Natural Illusions

Nature can be deceptive in many ways and at different levels of subtlety or obviousness. Rainbow colours appear to reveal the vibrant components of light, yet there is a far broader range of frequencies and wavelengths in light than we can visibly discern. The common assumption is that light is what enables us to see; the rest of the story eludes us. For example, birds have learned many ways to distract potential threats from their nests. Often the male bird acts as a decoy while the female lays still on the eggs, blending in with her surroundings, a trick which gives birds an advantage in order to survive. In fact, nature is full of deceptions and illusions.

Consciousness is the foundation of life that connects the unseen with the seen through light. Without light there would be no energy or the physical world. Our apparent world hides numerous levels of subtler forces, which are barely discernible or describable. Logic and causality are keys in describing what appears to us as real, but what is not apparent is of much greater magnitude, like the bulk of the hidden iceberg.

Consciousness is subtler than light and is at the root of existence and creation. There are countless ways of looking at consciousness and differentiating between its levels, spheres and spectrums. Two spheres stand out clearly, however. First is the basic level that makes human beings sentient and alive. This basic consciousness is the face behind the will to survive, grow, replicate, and so on. All living entities are energized by this consciousness. Human beings are distinct from other creatures due to a greater sphere of consciousness, which is higher consciousness, god-consciousness, supreme consciousness or soul consciousness. To this level belong all higher attributes and virtues such as mercy, generosity, forgiveness and others. Human ethics and morality evolve due to higher consciousness. To be like an animal at first is quite natural, but not to evolve and realize higher consciousness signifies an unfulfilled life. Every creation reaches its appropriate destiny when its highest potential (in terms of consciousness) is accomplished. God is the essence of universal supreme consciousness.

For a child it is natural and normal to be selfish and concerned mostly with its own physical sensory needs. With maturity comes the quest for a sustainable fulfilled life. The lights of higher consciousness begin to supersede the early 'survival' consciousness. To remain mainly bound to conditioned consciousness is to be deprived of awakening to the one real potential of soul essence. Our animalistic state of existence reinforces itself through multiple delusions, veils and worldly distractions, which divert us from accessing soul-consciousness.

If we look closely at all paradoxes and illusions, we see that they were in fact appropriate for us at a particular time or situation in this world, like the shell that protects the kernel of a nut. That is why it is said that there is goodness in everything that exists – if only we look with the eye of spiritual discernment. It is context and specific causality that needs to be viewed. A poison can kill and can cure. Egotism is essential in a child but out of season in a grown up and even detrimental.

Everything in nature reveals some aspects of itself and hides others. Everything earthly has also a heavenly aspect and every lie betrays an aspect of truth. To progress spiritually we need to witness naturally occurring illusions, assumptions and fallacies and break past them to the essence that is eternally constant and perfect.

1. Survival

Most animals, insects and other creatures use various ways of camouflage and deception to maximise their survival.

The survival instinct is paramount in all creation. The soul does not die and every self echoes that state. Life continues and every entity with a limited lifespan seeks longevity.

2. Ongoing Evolution

Just as biological evolution continues, so does consciousness.

Evolution is an endless process from unity via everythingness back to singularity. Natural physiological growth is accompanied by the growth of mind and consciousness.

3. Blind Spots

In nature, diversity and duality create a complex interactive world not easy to grasp as a whole. Thus, we focus on a particular direction and thereby miss many points along the way.

Realities are often masked by human emotions. A youngster in love will not see faults in the object of his affections.

4. Extending Boundaries

Within microbes, plants and animals the urge to procreate and extend personal and species domain is clearly evident.

The soul is boundless and every self or ego desires to occupy and dominate the earth, hence the plethora of species spread all over the earth.

5. Respect of Age and Distance

Long periods of time or distance, such as historical events or inaccessible mountain tops, seem to acquire the patina of sacredness.

The human soul originates from beyond space and time thus the self desires to be liberated from the restrictions of space and time and yet respect them.

6. Work in Progress

There is no meaningful finality or end to life since everything is in flux and subject to change. Yet we always look for closure and completion.

The soul is beyond space and time whilst the self on earth is on a quest for the permanent.

7. Sensory Illusions

All of our senses are subject to false prescriptions. Some of these include optical illusions such as the famous Kanizsa triangle, or auditory illusions in which an imaginary sound is heard, or tactile illusions such as phantom limbs. Why can't our senses always be true?

The soul does not see or hear; it just knows the truth. The self, comprising body, mind, intellect and heart, is being led to truth as known to the soul. During this process of evolvement, errors and faults are natural.

8. Eternal Life

We know that life doesn't end with personal death, yet we fear and regret death and consider it a calamity instead of a natural step forward.

The self is born into a world of space/time and acts as a veil to the eternal soul. With the realization of the sacred soul's presence, an enlightened person is liberated from the fear of death. There is only perpetual life in this world and beyond.

9. Orderly Chaos

With wisdom and science we discover order in every situation and event. With self knowledge, we also discover the reason behind physical and emotional chaos and confusion.

The soul is eternally in its perfect state and when the self focuses on higher consciousness and beyond limited identifications, it experiences harmony and contentment.

10. Seeking the Uncommon

It is a natural human tendency to seek and explore beyond the boundaries of the common and the familiar. The unknown on earth and beyond holds a strong fascination.

The restless self is in constant search for the boundless and absolute – the soul within. In the meantime, it follows the familiar pursuit of exploring the outer worlds!

11. Universal Symmetry

Everything in nature has its complementary or symmetrical opposite. There is no shadow without light, no inner without outer, no beginning without end.

Reflections and mirror-imaging are aspects of complementary duality. Eternal oneness has brought about natural diversity and two-ness, all of which point to their singular essence – One and Only One—every other illusion of special or independent oneness is merely echoing the truth of the sacred One.

Chapter 2

Personal Illusions

Life's numerous paradoxes, enigmas and apparent contradictions can be resolved when we consider the human being as a balanced composition between the self (conditioned basic consciousness) and a soul (pure consciousness). We may feel secure and content regarding an aspect of our life and yet at the same time apprehensive or insecure regarding something else. Even when one feels upbeat and happy there lurks a shade of sadness, due to the temporariness of this state. There is a subconscious fear of loss of the pleasurable moment as we have already experienced previous mood swings. No 'mental' state or feelings is ever lost. The swing between contentment and the desires continue.

Normal day-to-day human life contains countless illusions partly sensed and partly imagined or anticipated. The so-called 'real' life experiences are a result of a combination of subjective and objective factors, which in fact include fears, fantasies and wishful thinking. The ever-changing state of personal consciousness is dependent upon pure consciousness that permeates all existence. This sphere of constancy and wholeness engulfs and energises all lesser levels of consciousness.

Conditioned consciousness drives us to pursue whatever ensures survival, strength and growth and a host of other earthly needs. We naturally delude ourselves into pursuing extra desires and ideas superfluous to survival and basic stability. For example, love for wealth or power may relate to satisfying needs for physical survival and social status up to a point. Similarly body chemistry drives us towards sexual gratification and procreation but it often becomes a means to stimulate mental 'reward' chemistry. Through the power of hunger we are driven to act and know how and where to discover food and shelter. Ultimately, the drive to satisfy worldly needs leads to higher and subtler states of harmony and wellbeing at the levels of body, mind and heart.

Spiritual wisdom is the realisation that on its own the self/ego can never attain perfection or happiness. It is by transcending all illusions and so-called realities that we awaken to the ever-present Real. When the outer challenges lead to inner transformation, the joys of unity overflow beyond all that is seen and unseen.

12. Good or Bad Character

We tend to glibly label people as good, bad, brilliant or mediocre. In truth, there is no rigid personality, only changing traits, habits and behaviour.

The soul is always perfect and everyone strives towards perfection with varying degrees of consciousness of the soul that succeeds or fails – good or bad.

13. Guardian Angels

Many people believe they are protected by angels who guide and help. The idea of connection with the unseen realm has been with us from time immemorial! It seems we need this notion.

Intuition and subtle guidance occur reliably due to the purified self, which receives the soul's signals and light. The human soul is higher than all angels. The soul within the heart is not only the guardian and guide; it is the source of life.

14. Wealth and Poverty

Sometimes we may have outer wealth but feel inwardly impoverished and vice versa. More is not always better. Sometimes less is more!

If inner wealth is consistent then outer wealth or poverty hardly matter. The soul is beyond all measure of wealth and does not have an 'outer' or 'inner'. It is pure, unified light, and the self desperately seeks that.

15. Impartiality

Can we be objective, factual and unbiased in our experiences? No two people can relay facts about an event in exactly the same way.

The self and mind cannot be totally impartial or objective as there is no total separation between objectivity and subjectivity as they are perpetually relative. All experiences are based on relating the outer situation with the inner emotions and mental states.

16. Free Gifts

We enjoy receiving free gifts and winning the lottery. The self is always gratified with easy and free living.

Because the soul flows freely along perfectly and effortlessly, the self desires this state.

17. Surprise and Sameness

We enjoy pleasant surprises as well as the familiar and expected.

The self is very restless and seeks stimulation as well as calm and peace. The treasure of the inner soul is what it really searches for. All other pleasant surprises are short-lived.

18. Justification and Blame

It is a natural tendency to desire and expect whatever we consider acceptable and good and blame others for unrealised expectations.

The soul is ever-perfect and the self is like a shadow desiring perfection, which can only be attained by perfect submission to the inner master.

19. Perfect Destiny, Here and Now

We all desire to experience goodness now and in the future. We are always concerned about our destiny. But how can we ever be secure, sure and content?

'Perfect destiny' implies wellbeing and joy on a continuous basis. That state of bliss is also present now within the soul but we need to tune in to it. Disharmony in body or mind is the barrier to this state.

20. Flexible Self-Interest

All intentions and actions relate to self-interest – the lowest level of ego to the highest of selflessness.

Childish self-interest makes the ego grow. Wise self-interest indicates turning away from selfishness to 'soulfulness'.

21. Appearances

Most of us like to look good and wrinkle-free and yet it's a losing battle against nature.

The self wishes to appear as best as it can, in imitation of the soul – the ever-perfect. The purpose is the kernel, not the shell.

22. Youthfully Old

Most children prefer to be considered older than their age but the reverse is true of older people!

The self desires perpetuity which is a characteristic of the soul.

23. The Self as Schrödinger's Cat

Sometimes one feels alive beyond limits. At other times one is as good as dead. Are you alive or dead?

Ask the cat. The self is closer to death the moment it is born and the soul is ever-alive, so one is both alive and dead. An aspect of you is ever living, and another is dying.

24. Am I Needed?

We delude ourselves with justifications such as: 'they need me', 'I still have so much to do', 'there is still hope', 'I must not fail', 'I have a reputation to maintain', 'I have a duty', 'I can't let them down' and so on.

The very survival of the self and its evolvement depends on the above illusions. Life itself is eternally assured by the soul. And if the self and its activities and duties do not lead it to realise that the master was the eternal soul, then it will surely experience disappointment, irrespective of the outer success of the project.

25. Selflessness

Most human cultures and religions respect and honour acts of self-sacrifice and altruism. How can we reconcile love of the self with giving it up?

Initially the only love one knows is for the lower self. With evolvement of consciousness, we transcend identification with the body and mind and relate to the soul – thus selflessness.

26. Extreme Sport

Skydiving, bungee jumping, fear factor antics - it's a natural tendency to push the self to the edge.

The self is never content with worldly limitations, physical or otherwise. Relief and liberation will only be experienced when the self goes beyond all mental boundaries to the boundless soul.

27. Great Trophies

Prizes, cups and trophies - from childhood we seek acknowledgement. We encourage this trait even though it builds the ego.

The soul has all the prizes worth having and the self aims for this. During the early stages of our development we encourage the self/ego towards excellence. Wisdom will show us that the ultimate and perfect trophy lies within the heart. It is the soul that contains all the perfect qualities and prized traits.

28. Ever the Same

As a child, you use 'I' to describe yourself. In old age you use the same pronoun. Are you still the same?

Human beings are composed of an ever-changing self (body/mind/intellect) and a constant soul, which gives rise to the sense of sameness.

29. Dual Nature

Adventure vs. safety, the familiar vs. the unknown, accord vs. discord, love vs. hate, positive vs. negative, generous vs. mean – we exhibit infinite patterns of contradictions.

Whenever our thoughts and reflections are trapped within the limitations of the self and ego we are deprived of the energizing and positive qualities of the soul. The self is simply the dark side of all the great qualities of soul.

30. The Double-Edged Sword

We all struggle towards the good, and yet experientially we know whatever goodness exists often exists alongside its opposite.

Nature's knife is sharp on both edges. In this life everything is relative and changeable. Perfect goodness belongs to the soul.

31. Gender Superiority

Many men feel superior to women and equally many women may feel superior to most men. Who is greater then?

Each sex complements the other and evolves towards a higher state of wholesomeness and inner realization. Everything in life is in twos and oneness is the source behind all these dualities. Superiority can only mean ease of return to the One.

Chapter 3

Soul Searching

It is said that God has created the human soul in his own image. This soul therefore reflects all the divine attributes, qualities and knowledge. This metaphor also explains the saying, 'He who knows himself (the soul) knows his lord'. The self is composed of a lower ego and higher soul. By awareness and understanding the fickle nature of the ego-self, the higher self or soul consciousness begins to appear. Therein lies the divine light. Self-justification, defensiveness and prejudice are ways for the ego to assert itself during its evolvement. With maturity and insight we can transcend these early natural barriers and the soul's sanctuary within the inner heart will be realised.

Human beings need social interaction to survive and grow. Yet our own judicial systems punish a person by imprisonment and isolation. A monk or spiritual seeker undertakes voluntary isolation and confinement. By the same act of isolation one person is punished and made unhappy while another looks for relief, salvation and inner happiness. The punishment is for the ignorant who seek worldly distractions and feels deprived of them by force. Redemption is for the seeker who wants to reduce outer distractions in order to discover inner lights.

There is a natural order of priority in satisfying human needs. At first it is mostly sensory and physical, leading to subtler and intangible feelings and insights. The identity crises experienced at different stages during a young person's growth are expressions of confusion and insecurity about the meaning and purpose of life and the individual's place in it. However, we are all challenged by the question of 'Who am I?' followed closely by the question 'Where is my soul mate', or 'What will give me constant contentment or happiness?'

When outer friendship and union leads to inner harmony between self and soul and head and heart, then durable fulfilment is possible. Good relationships and outer compatibility can be a great step towards inner harmony and unity. Seeking outer harmony and 'good chemistry' are preludes to discovering the perfect mate within the heart.

The self is naturally addicted to the qualities of the soul: boundless contentment and eternally joyful. With wisdom, one discovers that what the self was looking for outwardly was ever resident within the heart. The self is like the musk deer: the faster it runs the more it is intoxicated with the odour of musk that is being emitted by its own gland! The darkest night heralds a bright dawn. Light and delight awaits those who listen, hear and connect.

32. The Perfect Mate Within

Most people nurture a notion that one day their ideal partner in life will appear. Where does this notion come from?

All of life's diversity emanates from unity. In essence every person is one. In order to realize that essential unity, life's experiences start with the self zigzagging its way towards the soul. Part of that practice is the human man-woman relationship. The 'outer two' reflect the 'inner twos'. With maturity and wisdom one sees that the real soul-mate was within one's heart all along and the worldly mate was a practice for that. Relationships represent complementary opposites seeking unity, when each partner helps the other to discover the eternal mate within the inner heart – the soul.

33. Eternally Loving

Everyone longs for permanent love yet human life is limited and has its ups and downs. From where does the notion of eternity emanate?

The soul's is a beatific eternal spark. It emits the original, sacred, unconditional love, which is the foundation of all creation. Every self, therefore, longs for that state.

34. God on Earth

It's quite natural for spiritual seekers to look for guides, saints, gurus or prophets. Yet we all know that God can never be seen. So what are we looking for?

The evolving self seeks reliable mirrors that may lead it to the path of union at heart. At best, a spiritual teacher is godly but fallible. God on earth is the spark of the soul within the heart.

35. Self- Affirmation

Every person, especially the young, enjoys being the centre of attention and being admired. With maturity, the wise person prefers humility and self-effacement!

Early on in life, the ego needs to grow and evolve. Later on it may learn that its essence is the noble soul and the self-ego is the veil and cover that needs to whither away before the inner light shines.

36. Restlessly at Peace

The self is naturally restless as it explores and searches for sustainable pleasures, ease and comfort. Yet we love peace, tranquillity and stillness.

The self is only a shadow of the perfectly contained and contented soul. The shadow flickers until it is aligned with its light – the soul. The outer movements are in perfect harmony with inner stillness.

37. Ego as Friend and Foe

It is often said, 'He who knows himself knows his Lord'. The real self is the soul and its reflection is the ego. How can we know ourselves?

What is necessary at the start of the journey (growth and evolvement of the ego) is the hindrance later on. Knowledge of the ego or lower self is through its restlessness and love for power and dominance. With wisdom and practice, one transcends towards the soul – the source of knowledge and power.

38. Soul Searching

We are driven to find the right connection, friendship and partner in life – the significant 'other'. Ultimately, all human desires relate to self-discovery.

The lower 'self' is always changing and can only rest with the constant soul. The self produces images projected upon the screen of the soul. That which perpetually changes can only be understood in relation to the constant.

39. Close to the King

We desire to be associated with powerful or famous people, yet we are touched at heart by the poor, sick or needy amongst the common folk.

The soul is noble, lofty and rules over the self, which is distracted by looking elsewhere for security and contentment. The self also enjoys being humble and generous and thus reduces its profile so that the light of the soul shines brighter.

40. Sharing Happiness and Grief

Pleasure taken at a spectacular sunset increases when shared. Sadness is reduced when shared.

Joy, bliss and happiness are energy fields which we can tap into and share when the conditions are right. The soul is in perpetual joy; and whenever we experience happiness the self is in unison with the soul. Inner goodness and light can be shared with others. Also shared grief lessens the self's insecurity and shock.

41. Incognito Celebrity

Famous people like to be recognised and occasionally blend like strangers in a crowd!

The ego-self enjoys status, recognition and admiration by others. Yet the self knows subconsciously that it isn't as it seems and that public admiration is short-lived, hence, the occasional desire to be ordinary and left alone. The self needs time and experience to progress toward the sanctuary of the soul – unseen yet the greatest treasure in creation.

42. Quest to Discover

Discoveries are endless so where is there closure?

The drive to gain knowledge and search for new discoveries remains strong in us throughout our life. A major change occurs when it turns from outer discovery to inner. The further you are from the source of light the more complex the shadows.

43. Success

It is natural for human beings to seek worldly success and power. Where is the limit to this endeavour? What is enough?

The soul rests within boundless wealth, knowledge and power. The self has taken on this complexion. But with its elusive nature it will never be content with the defined or the measured; it seeks omnipresence and omniscience.

44. Ultimate Destiny

At all times there is some apprehension about the future – 'What is my destiny?'

If that perfect inner state – enlightenment – is realized now, the ultimate destiny is already perfect.

Chapter Four

Common Fallacies and Paradoxes

Space/time is the crucible wherein life's mysterious alchemy of creation takes place. A moment in time contains a glimpse of eternity. The mystery of the absolute is veiled by the relative experience of the finite and of continuously changing events. The spiritual path bypasses time-related thoughts and leads to the boundless moment beyond conditioned or specific consciousness. Its destination is pure consciousness and the sacred realm of the soul.

It is the magic of space/time that produces all of the challenges, possibilities, as well as the paradoxes and contradictions in life. Infinity is veiled by the dynamics of beginnings and ends as part of complex interactions. Eternity hides behind every birth, which is naturally followed by death. All paradoxes, conundrums and contradictions disappear at the boundary of time or space where absolute Truth resides.

Space is the self's temporary, illusory home and time is the coach and teacher. The union of space and time produces countless separate identities nurtured and maintained for a while by the ever present cosmic source and essence of life.

We gain an understanding of the world through the use of our faculties of the outer and inner senses, especially the imaginal faculty, which evolves after birth, producing discernment, evaluation and distinction between matter, energies and forms. It is due to our senses that we can distinguish liquid from solid and experience the four dimensions of our earthly perch. During the early years of our life we learn how to cope with and exploit what is around us, through mind, reason, intellect and heart. Then come the more complex or perplexing questions regarding the meaning and purpose of life and death, suffering and pleasure, and other religious or philosophical issues.

People who meditate and practice accessing higher states of consciousness (including religious practices) often experience insights and openings that shed light on seemingly confusing or contradictory human situations and experiences. We all know that without water there would be no life on earth, yet polluted water is now a major cause of disease and death. Our life abounds in paradoxes of this sort.

Our natural love for peace, tranquillity and freedom are reflections of the state of the soul within the heart. Yet the self seeks excitement, change and attachments. These contradictions imply the simultaneous presence of two spheres of consciousness within us. One is conditioned and ever-changing while the other is pure soul consciousness. One level activates our physiological state and the other our spiritual and transcendental.

Studies of near death experiences indicate a state of consciousness beyond our day to day norm. Most religious teachings expound on life after death and attempt to prepare believers for that realm. The idea that 'life' continues after death seems to hold a natural appeal for most human beings and could be a reflection of the eternal nature of the soul rather than religious imagination.

Human evolution and the realization of higher consciousness takes place within our space and time-bound earth. So are our blockages of illusions, delusions and personal and collective confusions. The best and the worst are always connected. In truth, good and bad are born together in the world of change and relativity. The ultimate paradox is that human life is rooted in a world of interactive and relative states yet we constantly seek permanent goodness and happiness. Once this supreme paradox is dissolved all other conundrums and puzzles are resolved.

45. Ownership

'This is *my* house', 'She is *my* daughter', 'He is *my* father'. True or false?

In worldly relationships all these are true but temporarily so: the son can become a father, the house can be sold, and so on. In truth, no relationship is eternal. The self experiences worldly uncertainties and continues to look for security which is not attainable outwardly. The inner soul is ever secure and constant.

46. Limits of Knowledge

Scholars, scientists and sages agree with the wisdom that the more you know the more you realise how little you know!

There is no end to outer knowledge. The more we discover, the more there are new challenges for new discoveries. Inner knowledge and intuition has a different cosmology and belongs to another zone of consciousness – not measurable or limited.

47. Good Old Days

Is it regressive or simply selective memory that makes us regard aspects of the past as better than now?

The mind recalls special occasions in the past where the self felt good and its 'false' identity not challenged. In truth the past is neither better nor worse than now; it's all in the eye of the beholder, who relates and compares events in time rather than transcend to the presence of the ever-perfect soul.

48. Self before Others

Is it not wise to care for myself first and be secure and content before caring for others?

Outwardly each person is different whereas all the souls are the same. Pay less attention to the ego-self whose desires and demands are endless.

49. Beyond Old or New

We love new things - new clothes, new cars, new hairstyles - yet we treasure antique objects and old places as well as old customs and habits!

The self evolves by experiencing new events, tastes, feelings and knowledge. The soul is beyond time and age and contains the templates of what is considered new or old. Thus, both new and old are of no consequence as far as the eternal soul is concerned.

50. Near and Far

We love people and places that are near and familiar to us, yet we love to explore faraway places on earth.

The self is reassured by familiarity and yet it remains restless in its search for the elusive soul. We take for granted what is known to us and search for what is beyond – the soul.

51. Free at Last!

Although there is no such thing as total independence, we still seek freedom. Our life is meaningful because of ties that bind and yet we seek liberation from them!

All experiences in our life are relative and based on interdependence. Body, mind, intellect and heart, which constitute the self, are never totally free. Yet the self aspires for the same position as the soul, which is independent of any outer connection but drawing its energy from the cosmic soul.

52. Flexible Time

When we are in pain, time drags (expands); when we experience pleasure, time slows down (shrinks).

The self experiences life within space and time, whereas the soul is unrestricted by space or time. The self is impatient to be liberated from such constrictions by seeking oblivion or imaginary time travel. Human attempts to travel fast or delve deeply into the present moment (i.e. to end time) are attempts to break through the boundaries of space-time.

53. Differentiated Sameness

Most life experiences are based on differentiation and appropriate choices yet have arisen from one universal source of energy and life.

Everything in creation has an outer appearance and is identity based on energy. All different energy states have emanated from a single source and share sameness of origin. Before time everything was the same and so it will be after the end of time. All souls are the same in essence and all selves differ and change. All outer differences disappear when we consider the original inner sameness.

54. Fictional 'Always'

We say, 'I love you always', 'I am always here for you', 'you can always trust me', yet it is rare that these promises are totally fulfilled. Nothing is permanent!

The soul is beyond earthly limitations and is in sustained truthfulness. The self tries to be like that but cannot fully attain it in the outer world. The wisdom is that if you can't attain all goodness you don't abandon it all. Our uncertain world reflects an aspect of the real and true certainty.

55. A Long Way to Go

Wisdom often contradicts the natural human impulse for immediate gratification - thus tension!

The outer and the inner world are different but meet within the human being. On earth every event connects to others through multiple causes and effects and which are all subject to space and time. A tree needs several years to mature before giving fruit which ripen within a few days. The inner is timeless, and therefore instantaneous, and the outer has its worldly logic and laws. Wisdom prescribes appropriate reference between these two zones.

56. Medicating Depression

The root of depression and the love for oblivion coincide in obliteration of the self and supremacy of the soul.

There are naturally situations in which mind-altering drugs are unavoidable. The cause of all inner disturbance is due to lack of synchrony between mind, heart and ego/soul. Mental suffering is only an expression of inner discord energised by outer events. To address this clash we can take short-cuts and treat the symptoms or go deep into the roots of the situation. Outer medicine doesn't necessarily contradict the need for inner healing but does not always lead to that end.

57. Death Wish

Occasionally one may prefer to be dead. In the face of crises, we hide our face. The desire for oblivion during difficult or easy times is natural.

The self always looks for tranquillity, peace and goodness, yet it has to respond to the ever-changing worldly challenges. Ultimately relief or liberation comes from the extinction of the ego, either by unison with the soul while still in the body, or after death.

58. Friendship of Enemies

The heart is only purified when you can treat an enemy as a friend

All human souls are the same in essence but only outwardly are we different in countless ways. Friendship is in inner and outer harmony and trust. Enmity implies outer and inner discord and opposition. Everything in the outer world contains within it dualities. When the heart is pure, it is devoid of discord.

59. Money Solves All Problems

'If only I had enough money my problem would be solved!' – a winsome thought but doubtful.

In the material world, immediate, short-term needs can be helped with the power of money. You may access hearts and minds through the use of money but to maintain a state of inner tranquillity and contentment is something else. A gift may enable enemies to shake hands but for the relationship to last you need union at higher levels, such as with love of honesty, selflessness generosity and compassion.

Chapter Five

Obsessions and Addictions

A physical form is in essence energy caught for a while within apparent boundaries. The foundation of the universe is based upon the interchanging relationship between energy and matter and identifiable entities and an intangible reality. The origin of the whole universe is from an immense energy source that is beyond human measure or comprehension. This essence is   called God the Creator and the human soul is like its holographic represen-tation. The soul carries the imprints of supreme consciousness, which includes all the divine attributes and qualities. The self is the worldly shadow and companion of the soul and evolves towards this subtle and intangible life source. The heart is the abode of the soul and through it the self is inspired and drawn to its source. The human quest is based on the self's need to unite with its soul. The root of all human obsessions and addictions is this primal drive of the self/ego to be in the soul's abode, basking in divine grace. There is a driving passion in everyone to realise the permanent truth that resides within the heart.

The self's conditioned consciousness evolves through maturation of the mind, body, senses, emotions, reasoning and higher intellect. The child acts spontaneously and often inconsis-tently, illogically and restlessly. The young person's mind is trained to focus on issues and projects. The grown-up mind and intellect considers wider spheres of factors and influences that affect the issue under consideration. The wise and spiritually awakened person refers to the heart and soul seeking intuition or higher consciousness for a better reading and understanding of the situation.

Enlightenment is the outcome of unison between the self and

soul. The universal power of unity is in fact what holds the entire universe together. This unifying field is what drives the self or ego towards its inner caller - the soul within the heart. In fact, from the moment of its inception the human being is propelled to seek its true friend and companion within the heart. We are all addicted to reach our soul and merge into an unconditional sacred embrace. This state of inner unity and submission is the personal step towards the understanding of the universal state of divine unity and oneness.

Outer obsessions, addictions and distractions are side tracks from the imprint of the original innate self/soul obsession. We need to safeguard against all substitute, false and wayward addictions. The real addict is the self-soul unison which will be rewarded by living a rational and just life outwardly and constantly joyfully inwardly. The Sufis call this balanced and ultimate human state 'intoxicated sobriety' or complete human being.

60. Root of Addiction

We consider most obsessions and addictions to be detrimental, yet we cannot help ourselves.

In essence, the root of addiction is the drive of the self towards its ultimate objective - the soul. It is the diversion to other causes that is the problem. Obsession with reference to higher consciousness is most admirable. The futility lies in being obsessed with earthly pursuits.

61. Key Obsessions

Power, knowledge, wealth, ability, skills, status, popularity, ownership and control etc. Why do we lust after them?

These are the soul's attributes, considered good or positive and the self loves to possess them.

62. Forbidden Fruit

The illicit is often compelling.

The self always desires to be free of limitations. The rational mind can regret a wrong action, whereas testing the limits is natural for self-evolvement. It could lead to new and valuable experience or to some regret. Our world always imposes limits but the self desires the limit-lessness of the soul.

63. Vice and Virtue

Most normal people know what is good or bad in any given situation. Also, we know that sometimes a good action can have the opposite results.

All vices belong to the self, all virtues to the soul. Awareness of a vice can lead to a change of attitude and behaviour to the virtue, which is its opposite. A virtue out of context can become an unexpected vice – such as kindness to a cruel despot.

64. Oblivion through Drugs

We enjoy deep sleep. Some people enjoy intoxication through drugs or alcohol. Yet we also know the importance of health and alertness!

The self is energized by two levels of consciousness. One gives us individuality and conditioned awareness and the other sphere is higher consciousness that takes away from the limitations of ego and self to the freedom of the soul. Drugs give us temporarily a window to this blissful state with a heavy price of side effects. It is only through self-knowledge and spiritual transcendence that we attain durable joy and enlightenment.

65. Seeking Approval

Throughout our life we enjoy acknowledgement and being regarded as special. The self and ego is enhanced by anything that reinforces self importance!

Intrinsically the fact that the soul is still within us and has not departed signifies approval and love. Yet we want to be free from people's opinions. The wise seeker cares less for the self and its desires and more for the purity at heart and access to the soul. The soul is loved and approved eternally and the shadowy self wishes to emulate it unjustly.

66. Obsession with Possession

It is a common trait to accumulate objects and other belongings. Owning the whole Earth may still not be enough.

The soul is exposed to the knowledge of wealth beyond measure, and the self desires that.

67. The Desire to Belong

People seek their roots and want to belong – to a family, tribe, nation, football club or whatever. It enhances the sense of identity, worldly presence and security. We need to belong and yet at times resent it.

The restless self needs to consciously know that it belongs to the soul. Initially it desperately seeks freedom and independence – peace and harmony is the result of self-soul unison.

68. Good Enough!

No extent of wealth, power, knowledge or fame will fully satisfy any individual.

The self is driven to higher consciousness via oblivion of the discernable world that is the soul's abode. The soul is exposed to the boundless fields of energy representing power, knowledge and all other desirable attributes and treasures and the self seeks these on earth with natural limitations – thus not good enough!

69. Keeping and Revealing Secrets

We like to have special secrets and yet we enjoy solving puzzles or uncovering mysteries or secrets.

The soul is the ultimate sacred secret and inner treasure that the self needs to discover and be content. The earth is the training ground for this supreme discovery.

70. Elusive Contentment

We always look for the best, most stable ultimate 'permanent' home, occupation, friendship, independence, security, love and freedom — without any lasting success!

All outer challenges and desires are indications for the primal desire of self-soul unison and peace.

71. Seeking Truth

Everything in our world is relative, including truth and falsehood, yet we still want the ultimate truth!

The self is alive because of the light of the soul. Spiritual progress is from relative truth to the universal absolute truth that permeates the seen and the unseen. This truth is eternal and is ever-present (in reduced strength) within every moment and situation. The self, however, will progress with relative truth seeking the ultimate, constant and absolute which is the quality of the soul.

72. Immortality

We love to be remembered and missed by those whom we love. We also like to have our legacy or works to continue after our death.

The body returns to dust and the soul carries on into the realm of higher consciousness. This is where the notion of posterity comes from.

73. Falling in Love

A person in love is distracted, light-hearted or deliriously happy, albeit for a short while. Flight of fancy or helpful experience?

When in love, the ego is reduced and the 'other' person is given more attention than the usual personal selfishness – thus the temporary elation. The self is restlessly looking for its permanent soul-mate; the act of falling in love is a faulty trial, which merely recalls the approximate state of realizing the true inner love affair with the soul.

Chapter 6

Collective Illusions

The human being is a complex social animal whose evolution depends largely upon family, society and cultural norms. Nurture is as much to do with parenting as with the extended family, tribe or nation. A personality is an ever-changing product of genetic inheritance influenced by early childhood, habits and the environment. To belong to a group larger than the immediate family is an essential factor in human survival as well as in growth and progress in life skills, civilization, politics, economics, religions, moral values, and other issues which produce a better quality of life and evolvement of consciousness. Group or societal influences are key to personal behaviour and value systems. The power of the collective is often underestimated and is difficult to understand or control, i.e. social behaviour is much deeper and more complex than we think.

Survival of the fittest implies the physical, mental as well as spiritual (higher consciousness) in the case of human beings. Altruism and sacrifice for the common good is an important human habit and it is firmly entrenched in most cultures and behaviour. Acknowledgement of heroes and outstanding members of a society or nation is an integral part of pride in identity, belonging and bonding within groups. For thousands of years the human mind and past memories reinforce the importance of being accepted by a clan or social group. Cultural habits, fashion, economic activities, religion, leisure, politics and other human endeavours and outer social factors affect every individual within that culture as well as other people who interact with it.

Thus no matter how strong-willed or independent-minded an

individual may appear to be, there will always be some influence caused by others. In our present time the effect of the media, the internet and global trade can be traced in almost every person in the world. Therefore it is almost impossible for anyone to think or act totally independently of others beyond the close geography. The collective mind cannot be dismissed from the personal psyche, thoughts, actions and values. Changes in personal perspective and social norms always interact to produce a modified outcome. Social values and collective habits are much harder to change than personal ones. Changes and reforms in religious beliefs and rituals are always slow and difficult to bring about in a large group of people. We enjoy traditions and familiarity of repetition of past collective acts. To eradicate superstitions or other detrimental habits is not easy even when the advantage in their removal is demonstrated. A society has a 'mind' of its own and can be most illogical and unreasonable to the 'individual mind'. Mass revolt or hysteria has its own dynamics and reason beyond 'normal' reason.

During upheavals, calamities and suffering the collective and past habits and ideas seem to surface stronger than before. Group delusions seem to act as stress and pressure relief when we are in difficult or hopeless situations. The expectation of the arrival of the messiah or saviour increases with suffering and despondency. Collective illusions often override individual reason and wisdom. This is why prophets are almost always denied by their own people. Group attitude and habits bestow extra stability and security to its members. Collective norms and illusions are common to all of mankind and manifests distinctively according to different cultures and societies. People often seek refuge in the familiar even though it is of no real use or it is even counter-productive. Individuals and groups always seek the elusive security and safety that can only be tapped inwardly before outer experience. We always think by fixing the outer world that the inner will be in harmony. The truth is the reverse of this notion.

74. Sanctified by History

Historical events and commemoration make people feel proud and secure!

As the soul is timeless and ever-secure, the self feels good about antiquities and its connection with early historical occurrences. Collective minds find history and old traditions comforting as it gives the illusion of continuity.

75. Aggressively Peaceful

Many countries talk much about peace but follow hawkish rulers with eagles perched on their flags.

Conditioned consciousness relates to aggression and biological survival. Peace, compassion, generosity and all higher attributes relate to pure consciousness, which relates to spiritual evolution. Aggression is a primitive and primal characteristic in humans but love of peace is an inner and subtler trait which needs to be cultivated.

76. Mind of Society

People are often described as open-minded or close-minded

It is natural to be close-minded. The nature of the mind is to contain and limit and delineate things, whereas the heart is boundless and everything is possible in its domain. Open-mindedness implies connectedness with an open heart.

77. Time Matters

We often quote: *'quality time, just in time, no time left, end of time, time's up, give me more time, time flies when you're having fun, time stopped, time heals, time waits for no man, race against time, time, no time to lose...'*

As long as we function with conditioned consciousness, time and space is our home and everything is measured accordingly. Only when higher consciousness is referred to do we realise the illusions of life on earth.

78. Space Matters

What do we really mean by: 'far away, close by, no way to reach, huge mountain, tiny speck, outer space, atomic space, infinite, finite'?

Our terrestrial father and mother are space/time and we are bound by their rules, which we want to break free from – as the soul is.

79. Conformity

Conformity reduces the challenge and uncertainty of change.

The self always seeks stability. Repeated patterns of behaviour enhance the illusion of ongoingness. Individuals may be flexible but group dynamics teach the child to always follow a set pattern.

80. I and We

Both psychology and sociology are needed to reflect individual and collective behaviour.

Like all dualities they are inseparable. If you start life's quest to discover who you are, you will end up with who they or we are. There is dependency and mirroring in all societal settings.

81. Collective Honour

An individual may practice self-effacement and humbleness, but for a group, status and honour is more dominant!

For an individual, it is easy to realise that higher consciousness is accessible through humbleness and abandonment of ego. For a group, however, the show of power and status has been important for survival and dominance for millennia.

82. Unique but Ordinary

Everyone needs to belong to a family, tribe, society or profession. Yet each person hopes to be special and recognized as unique

All human souls are the same (special and unique) and the self strives for the same high status. Every person is uniquely different in an outer sense and is the same in essence.

83. Triumphalism

The public enjoy participating in great national events and pageantry. The crowd, the noise and the commotion adds to the atmosphere!

Life's quest is fulfilled when the self triumphs over itself. The cult of heroism and mass hysteria during national celebrations and sporting events are to do with the lower collective self. The louder is the noise, the less is the likelihood of the self reflecting upon the illusion of the event.

84. Feared or Loved

Usually we either fear or love a thing.

The self loves whatever enhances it and acknowledges its reality and fears whatever reduces the ego. Initially the soul (God or teacher) is feared and avoided by the self. With wisdom and spiritual insight, the person acts against the ego as a matter of course and the teacher is then both loved and feared.

85. War and Peace

We place a high value on peace yet seem to war more often.

When the inner conflict between ego and soul is minimized, outer conflict will also lessen. Discord and aggression continues until conditioned consciousness is submerged by higher consciousness or until the self has yielded to the soul.

86. Family Quarrels

Every family experiences discord, jealousy and animosity, yet everyone expects and hopes for harmony and goodwill and generosity.

Animosity and aggression are among the essential traits of the lower self that relate to basic survival and dominance and almost all children will show some measure of these traits early on. When the self has been made reasonably secure, then higher consciousness begins to influence behaviour. Love of power and gold is superseded by the love for the all powerful god. The desire for personal power is a prelude to recognition of the All-powerful. The self seeks gold until it realises the light of God within its heart.

87. Ancient Culture

We are pleased and proud when we discover our ancient roots.

The soul is before time and the self wants to replicate that. The collective self also feels pride and power in being early on the earthly scene. Security and timelessness is always sought after.

Chapter Seven

Higher Illusions

Almost every human being thinks they are extra special, unique and deserves particular acknowledgement, recognition and a happy life. Most groups of people, societies and nations consider themselves better than others at least in some aspects. This 'God chosen' illusion is an echo of the 'god sent' soul within us. The soul is a sacred treasure within the heart and is at the root of the perpetual human quest for outer treasures, precious and rare finds. It is naturally easier to look for outer gems than to focus upon the discovery of the inner soul and its microcosm.

Any activity or interest that makes one pay less attention to the self or ego is somewhat alleviating. The less of lower consciousness, the greater is the possibility of higher consciousness, awareness and openings. Being less self concerned brings about a certain elation, freedom and pleasure. To 'give' to others is to 'receive' in return. The root of all love is the primal love of the self for its soul reflecting God's love for all of creation. All other loves and passions are insignificant compared to this original and unconditional love. Love is the universal glue which connects and unifies diverse entities. It is the cosmic field where all opposites return to complementarity and unity.

Religious, moral or metaphysical beliefs and practices often produce good feelings and a subconscious sense of superiority, elevation or 'special' status. To admire the self and ego in a worldly sense is a bad enough delusion but to bestow upon oneself an elitist religious or spiritual status is a great obstacle to the realisation of higher consciousness. Sometimes the 'righteous' ego of the religious 'person' is more difficult to overcome and subdue than the simple selfish and worldly ego. To change a recognized bad habit or a vice is easier than getting rid of pride or superior feelings due to good acts, worship, piety or admired virtues. Meanness may lead a person to realize the selfish nature of the lower self and thus change behaviour towards generosity. But seeing oneself as 'generous' or 'pious' is more difficult to deal with. When religion is used for worldly purposes and power, it can be more damaging and dangerous than the usual worldly business, desires and greed – structured religion can produce obstacles and distractions for real spiritual progress if not practiced for inner transformation.

Higher delusions are stubborn and often require a major shock to break the old edifice of personal values and habits. To work for 'God's sake' and serve humanity or other popular causes may give a person a certain position, status and reputation which can obstruct the path of inner sublimation and enlightenment. God does not need anyone to serve him. It is only divine grace that enables us to act less selfishly and more generously towards others. But once pious and virtuous deeds become a person's profession and part of a personality, image or reputation then the self and ego is deluded beyond easy correction. This false state of 'sanctity' is out of harmony with creational balance between opposites (the despicable ego and the sacred soul) and will lead to a greater disaster which often accompanies religious pride and arrogance. Higher or religious delusions are the most complex and difficult to overcome.

The soul is always 'high' the self is 'low' and human nature oscillate between these two polarities representing good and bad behaviour. It is thus natural for the self or ego to aspire to the soul and it is a self-delusion when it imagines 'itself' to be high or glorious. The self or ego is always despicable and the soul is always sacred. The more the self is subdued and is humbled the more the soul may shine over the whole person. It is said that God honours those who humble themselves and will debase those who are proud.

88. By Faith Alone

Faith and trust help the evolving self to reach the abode of timeless presence.

Faith can be a hollow word or it can be a door that leads to new states of consciousness. You may imagine a message from God and someone else may hear exactly the opposite. Religious discord and warfare have accompanied us for as far as we can recall. Faith and trust in God or a supreme hand or higher consciousness can help to connect self to soul and head to heart.

89. Fallacy of the Pure Person

We often equate goodness with purity. We call prophets and saints pure beings! What about the decaying bodies?

The soul is pure and reflecting pure consciousness. The self is naturally conditioned and impure. Every human being is composed of a pure (soul) and a contaminated (self). A saint is a human being who is consistently aware of the soul (or God) without denying the earthly body on earth.

90. Fate and Fatalism

Ignorant people do not accept personal responsibility for their life and end up as fatalistic.

Intelligent man does his best whilst reconciling and accepting outcomes beyond one's control. A rational being tries to read the events and respond to them appropriately. The ultimate outcome is considered as acceptable fate by the rational wise person who reads beyond the actual outer events and witness's perfection in causalities and interaction in creation.

91. Religions today

On balance religions have helped humanity in bringing about higher values in behaviour as well as stable relationships and transactions between people.

Religions have played a crucial role in shaping human cultures and civilisations for the past four to five thousand years. Religions have helped to establish basic ethical and moral standards and norms. They were also used to enforce control and conformity amongst people and played a big role in bonding diverse ethnic groups. In our times, structured religious authority is losing ground to people's need of spiritual openings and access to inner guidance and inspiration. The self needs to be groomed and restrained in order for the soul to transmit its eternal message of oneness.

92. One God, Multiple Creations

It is wisely said that there are as many paths to God as there are human beings.

By transcending the lower self we realize that creation is held by immutable divine powers and attributes. Our world is experienced as the interchange between two opposites and that the human make-up is balanced between head and heart, or ego and soul. As God is the absolute one essence behind all of creation then there are as many pathways to God as there are creations. In truth there is only God that exists and all creations are emanations from that essence. The soul is like a spark from the divine light and the self is its shadow.

93. Good Deeds

Religious morality and good deeds are often based on helping and serving others in any way that reduces suffering, compassion or the lack of purpose in life!

Higher consciousness and the desirable qualities of patience, generosity and love all emanate from the soul within the purified heart. Most good deeds and selfless acts of sacrifice purify the heart and will help one to be a better human being. The danger is self-righteousness and religious arrogance.

94. Spiritual Progress

If pure consciousness is beyond time, then what is the meaning of spiritual progress?

You sometimes hear people comparing notes as to who is spiritually higher in status. This is spiritual materialism or a business camouflaged in religion!

Human beings are a composition of higher (soul) consciousness and its shadow or image, called self-consciousness. Spiritual progress is the connection of these spheres of consciousness and thereby giving reference and direction to the self.

95. Religious Miracles

We are fascinated by magic and miracles.

We never cease seeking them. The desire for miracles is to reassure the self of the possibility of the discovery of the ultimate miracle – the soul within. The ultimate miracle is timelessness in time, mortality as a glimpse of immortality. When there is no desire within the self then the carpet of destiny unfolds easily for that being.

96. Paradise Club

Most religious people think that they are right in their belief or religion. Some even think they are exclusive in being the 'chosen people'! Where then is divine justice and love of God for all creation?

The self always looks to enhance itself and attain ultimate salvation. To experience paradise on earth and especially within one's own heart, one is more ready for eternal paradise. The soul is most favoured by God as it contains the divine qualities and knowledge. The self wishes this special privilege and honour. The collective self of a group also wishes the same!

97. Eradicating Poverty

There is a common human wish to end poverty, yet this goal seems to be increasingly elusive.

As everything in creation is one of two, poverty is the dark side of wealth and riches. Also wealth and poverty are outer as well as inner. To reduce outer poverty we also need to increase the awareness of inner richness (of the soul). Without this balance we will only experience failure. Some people are rich outwardly and poor at heart. Others are the opposite; rich at heart and poor in the worldly sense. A few are rich in both domains.

98. Blessed are the Meek

Sometimes you find simple folks are happier and more content than the more sophisticated!

There is a vast difference between being content with little and being covetous and constantly wanting more. Historically meekness meant that the elite and wealthy considered the poor and needy as meek. Generally the less outer desires and needs the more one is potentially free to realize inner wealth and contentment. When there is inner ease and peace, then the soul and higher consciousness are dominant in life – thus blessed!

99. Elixir of Youth

Why are we humans obsessed with the issue of immortality?

The soul is immortal and the self yearns for that. Once it is ready to give up its illusion of separateness then we realize that there is only immortality. In truth, there is only God and everything else is an overflow of the cosmic soul – all of creation is a shadow of that truth.

100. Father or Mother in Heaven

What is the origin of the notion that we'll be saved by sacred beings somewhere or somehow?

Since the self has grown accustomed to the physical and material earthly life, it imagines its spiritual life in earthly familial terms. It is easier to imagine salvation by a heavenly father than an abstract God or supreme consciousness – thus personalization!!

101. The Punishing God

Most people consider God as the most compassionate and loving, yet we also sometimes think that God punishes people for sins!

God has created all of the known and the intangible entities and realities in the universe according to patterns and laws that connect and interact harmoniously. We human beings fit in life on earth as part of its wholeness and all pain and suffering is a warning sign of undue transgression, and thus a sign of mercy and compassion. By correct attitude, intention and action, the so-called punishment will be seen as a reminder to take heed and change behaviour. God is only perfect and merciful and has created us to recognise and 'worship' those qualities.

Chapter Eight

Illumined Conclusions

Most human beings desire and hope for sustainable happiness. As a result we think reason and act in the hope of health, wealth and well-beingness in body, mind, and heart. These are primal drives for all times.

Our human ancestors wondered about, reflected upon and speculated about time, destiny, death and the hereafter. 'Is there life after death?' has been a perennial question. If there is some consciousness after death how can we be prepared for it? As most of us strive towards worldly happiness or joy, much of our energy is consumed by daily challenges, even though we know that worldly experiences are transient and swing between opposites. With remembrance of death a wise person becomes more concerned with the inner state rather than outer worldly issues.

One helpful model of human nature is the one that was propagated (with variations) by many ancient and classical philosophers, thinkers as well as prophets, religious leaders, wise sages and enlightened beings. This model is based on duality rooted in unity. Its foundation is that a person is composed of both physical and material aspects interacting by means of subtle energy networks (electromagnetic and vibrational) to produce physical and chemical changes. The source of life energy is a non-discernable soul or spirit. The human being comprises of worldly or earthly dimensions as well as a mysterious spiritual aspect. When these two states work in unison the result is a natural, healthy and authentic person. Otherwise physical, chemical or psychological imbalances show up in acute or chronic fashion. A classical example for balance between two entities is that of the left and right brain hemispheres. The left is the base of reason and rationality whilst the right is where intuition or higher consciousness lies. We need both for a healthy life. We are both heavenly and earthly. We are stardust infused by the light of timelessness.

Practical difficulties and countless stresses and contradictions face us throughout our life. Most of these can be understood if we refer to the model of self and soul within us and recognize the hierarchy of needs. The human self is conditioned consciousness and is essential for survival whilst higher consciousness is there always to propel us towards the boundless and eternal state which is inherent within the soul. The self will remain ever restless until it resonates (obeys!) with its inner call of essence (soul or spirit), which reflects the universal soul or divine reality and truth.

Reflect upon how the self desires contentment while the soul is ever content. The self seeks to control while the soul is in control. The self tries to lead while the soul is the perfect leader. The self depends upon others and desires to be depended upon while the soul has no needs. The self desires to heal and be healed whereas the soul is ever-intact and wholesome. The self desires to give and receive whereas the soul only gives energy and life. The self seeks to protect and be protected whereas the soul is ever safe and secure. The self desires to be respected by others whereas the soul is ever honoured by God. The self desires to guide and be guided while the soul is ever-knowing.

Consider the following situations with the self-soul model as a reference:

On the search for freedom and security: Why do we always seek freedom and yet never find it? That is the perpetual story of the self—it wants to be free and yet it gets trapped in worldly situations. Liberation implies surrendering to the soul; and by so doing one is free from all of these illusions. In spite of our love for freedom we perpetually get entangled in ties that bind us further. In the world of causality and duality there is no outer sustainable freedom. An evolved self will look inward for salvation while putting up with endless outer challenges. Even when you are in a heavy duty prison, you can enjoy endless freedom at heart. We love the idea of independence (the romance of the desert island) whilst realising life is based on interdependence (no man is an island). The earth is the zone of interdependence. The human quest for independence reflects the illusion of the self that it is independent of the soul. A child grows from dependence on its parents to apparent independence. A wise being realises higher dependence, otherwise old age will bring despondence. How can one be certain and secure in this life? The self as such is always restless as a shadow and can't be safe or secure for any length of time. By abandoning our clumsy attempts at outer permanent security, we may increasingly access inner certainty and contentment at heart.

On feeling self-important: Everyone wants to be someone special even though that state cannot be maintained for long. As long as we have the strong identity of a particular self we will experience distance from the self-soul unity. It is the soul that is truly important and the self desires that acknowledgement. Almost everyone thinks themselves to be special or that their talent will one day be discovered. The self and ego are concerned with acknowledgment and admiration whereas the mature person realises that it is the soul that is real and admirable while the self is merely the shadow.

On falsehood: Every appearance in life has some falsehood and fallibility – yet we always seek absolute truth. When absolute truth appears in a changing world it instantly becomes relative and will always be accompanied by some falsehood. It's all a matter of quality and quantity. This state is reproduced by self-soul relationships. The soul is perfect and true and the self   is the shadow on its way to unison. We resent falsehood and yet we often conceal what we consider unattractive outwardly (cosmetics) and inwardly (hatred). The self desires the perfection of the soul and thus concealment and outer falsehood. The light of truth from the soul makes us normally resent lies, dishonesty and falsehood. Does saying 'to be honest' imply that what you said earlier was dishonest? Indeed the self lies and is often dishonest. Truth is constant and honesty implies that the self is in reference to the soul. The ultimate honesty and truth meet at the cosmic soul.

On self-denial: It is natural for the self to accuse others as being the cause of anger, pettiness, meanness, greediness, aggressiveness, sadness, arrogance, despair, pessimism, immorality, anxiety, apathy, fanaticism, disloyalty, vengefulness, disagreeableness, indifference, dishonesty and other negative traits. The self-ego is a shadow and veil over the soul. It is energized by the inner light and its purpose is to submit to and unify with its essence. Due to identification with the body and mind, the self becomes identified and independent and denies its reliance on the soul. If the self recognizes that it is embodying such negative qualities it may change and move on to the positive side. But since the self wants the constancy of the soul, it keeps denying it is perpetrating a wrong doing or vice and it justifies itself that it is better than others.

On consumer culture: People enjoy being surrounded by luxury and consume expensive food and drink because the self loves to be pampered and is never satisfied. The ultimate luxury in existence is the knowledge of the most precious jewel residing in one's own heart. The self or ego is regarded as a beast in some cultures and religions and yet it is natural to be selfish. The self can be beastly if it is not groomed and trained to refer to the heart. Understanding other animals and their behaviour implies that we possess their pattern within us. In fact, the human soul contains the design of all other souls.

On medical authority: We make ourselves sick and often heal ourselves — yet we seek outer doctors and physicians. When we are confused, we seek expert advice to relieve us from our suffering. Hoping to be in good hands is natural. In truth, the best of hands are one's own. Other people may lend a hand but ultimately it is one's own responsibility regarding actions and choices. The soul within can transmit its healing power when the heart is purified.

On being religious: Some religiously pious people seem to be less attractive than worldly egotistic ones. Why? The pseudo religious person desires holiness. We all know that the sacred is subtle and once it manifests then it is subject to the duality of good and bad. The religious self justifies its own cosiness rather than the intended abandonment to the cosmic self. Religion is much abused for worldly power and status. Some say that we have to renounce this world to attain the next. All worldly knowns and unknowns have emanated from the one source which permeates them all. It is only about emphasis and balance rather than renunciation. This world can be an easy stepping stone for spiritual progress and could also be a burial ground with no further progress. When the outer leads to the inner and connects the two domains then heavens and earth meet within us. What is the reason behind our quest for purity, even though life on earth is never pure as it is based on numerous ingredients? Absolute purity is only in essence and has given rise to all the cocktails of creational realities. So in the outer world the quest for purity is relative and if it doesn't lead to inner channelling of pure soul then it will disappoint. Religious belief and convictions can increase as well as reduce human strife and warfare. They say the problem is bad religion and the solution lies in good religion. But who will decide what is bad and good? Religions or spiritual paths are there as a map to help the self attain unison with the soul, otherwise they are distractions and distortions.

On perfect moments: What is the nature of epiphany or spiritual insights? The ultimate human experience involves all the cells in the body and transcends all the senses and awareness. It can bring about exhaustion as well as strength. A peak experience is an example of temporary unison between self and soul. How to realise that the instant or moment is immense and eternally perfect? The soul is ever-perfect and the cosmic soul/ God is the source of all perfection but veiled by what is imperfect. The illusion of imperfection drives us to interaction in the world and share in the divine miracle of creation. When we reflect deeply on the moment in time and go beyond all sensation we are at the edge of utter perfection. Death brings about the sudden realization of this.

* * *

Human morality, higher values and virtues belong to the spheres of consciousness. Basic consciousness is limited to the individual and is subject to evolutionary dynamics such as natural selection, survival, growth and procreation. This personal and conditioned consciousness energises the human ego and personal identity as in body, mind and senses and evolves as one grows older. The other dominant sphere of higher consciousness is all pervasive, universal and supreme and is the cause for all levels of consciousness and life. The soul is an offshoot of this supreme consciousness and is the cause of the self, ego, body, mind and heart. Our link with supreme consciousness (or God) is via the soul within the heart. For this reason most religions aim at purifying the heart so that the light of the soul illumines the mind and other faculties of the self.

The ultimate purpose of life is to recognise the need for resonance between head and heart (self and soul) and to realise the unity of conditioned and pure consciousness. True contentment arises when all earthly dualities and different dimensions are seen through the eye of unity. This unifying insight brings about durable harmony and joy. Distractions from this enlightened state produce countless illusions, falsehoods and disappointments. The desire for bliss, paradise and eternal happiness is indeed the most powerful drive in human life. The state of joy on earth is found according to the extent of our ability to transcend our historical, evolutionary and mental limitations. Most spiritual practices aim to take us past 'natural' thought state to a higher sublime zone of consciousness. We need to overcome the barrier of words and language and simply experience insights and lights transmitted by the purified heart as beams of pure consciousness. The realisation of the absolute truth of the ever perfect and eternal presence of the one essence is enlightenment. Many other names are given to this transcendent state, which in itself has levels and spectrums. What is the ultimate conclusion of this journey on earth? To reach the proper conclusion in any situation we need first to set aside personal illusion. When the self realises all its illusions and virtual realities then it may end up in the abode of perpetual trust and joy within the heart. Surely that is the most appropriate conclusion?

Meanings and purposes which we give to personal life are useful for evolvement until we realize that the ever-perfect source of life (Soul, God or pure consciousness) was actually veiled behind all the human thoughts, purposes and meanings. The real purpose of human life is to interact with all the forces in creation, realise the temporariness and illusion of all experiences and then transcend to the constant presence of the eternal perfect light within. The truth will then be known as boundless, eternal and all-encompassing. There was always the ONE and all twos are driven to return to unity and be at peace ever after.

BOOKS

O is a symbol of the world, of oneness and unity. In different cultures it also means the "eye," symbolizing knowledge and insight. We aim to publish books that are accessible, constructive and that challenge accepted opinion, both that of academia and the "moral majority."

Our books are available in all good English language bookstores worldwide. If you don't see the book on the shelves ask the bookstore to order it for you, quoting the ISBN number and title. Alternatively you can order online (all major online retail sites carry our titles) or contact the distributor in the relevant country, listed on the copyright page.

See our website **www.o-books.net** for a full list of over 500 titles, growing by 100 a year.

And tune in to myspiritradio.com for our book review radio show, hosted by June-Elleni Laine, where you can listen to the authors discussing their books.

MySpiritRadio